The Body

Lungs

Veronica Ross

Chrysalis Children's Books

First published in the UK in 2004 by
Chrysalis Children's Books,
An imprint of Chrysalis Books Group PLC
The Chrysalis Building, Bramley Road, London W10 6SP

ISBN 1 84458 093 8

British Library Cataloguing in Publication Data
for this book is available from the British Library.

Editorial manager: Joyce Bentley
Editors: Rosalind Beckman, Joe Fullman
Illustrator: Chris Forsey
Designer: Wladek Szechter
Picture researcher: Jenny Barlow

Printed in China

10 9 8 7 6 5 4 3 2 1

Words in **bold** can be found in Words to remember on page 30.

Picture credits
Angela Hampton/Family Life Picture Library: FC (Inset) 5, 9, 14, 18, 19, 21, 22, 24, 26.
Chrysalis Images/Ray Moller: 1, 4, 15.
Corbis: Nancy Ney 8; Jennie Woodcock/Reflections Photolibrary 10;
Jose Luis Pelaez, Inc. 11;
Jack Hollingsworth 13; Alan Jakubek 27.
Ecoscene: Jeff Collett FC (Main) 17; Angela Hampton FC (Inset), 25.
Getty Images: Julia Fishkin 20.
Science Photo Library: GUSTO FC (Inset), 7.
Illustrations: Chris Forsey 6, 12, 16, 23, 28, 29, back cover (inset).

Contents

Look at me!

I can blow up a balloon. I can see my breath on a cold day. My **lungs** allow me to do these things. They take in air and allow me to **breathe**.

Breathing is one of the most important things your body does. The air that you breathe in keeps you alive.

When you blow a dandelion clock, air is forced out of your lungs and through your mouth in a huge whoosh.

Where are my lungs?

You have two lungs inside your chest. They are protected by the **bones** that make up your **ribcage**.

Your lungs are like two soft, pink sponges.

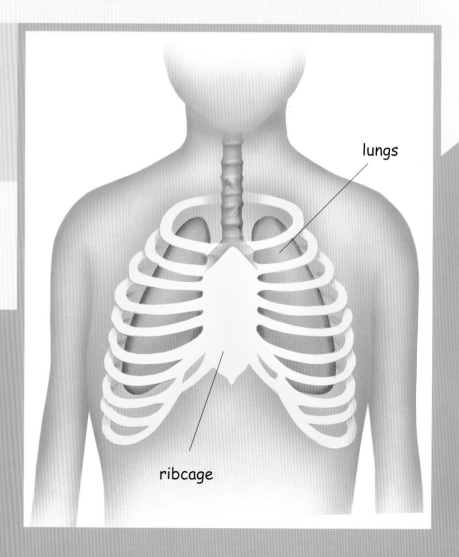

lungs

ribcage

The ribs go around the lungs to keep them safe. Your lungs are so big that they take up most of the space in your chest.

Your lungs hold about 2.5 litres of air. That's enough to blow up a balloon.

What do my lungs do?

Your lungs allow you to breathe. They take in fresh air and get rid of **stale** air. They do this all day, every day.

You breathe when you eat, when you talk and when you are asleep.

You breathe in and out all the time without thinking about it.

The air that you breathe out is used for talking.

A newborn baby takes about 40 breaths a minute. You breathe about 25 times each minute.

Why do I need to breathe?

You need to breathe in air to stay alive.

A gas called **oxygen** is in the air we breathe.

Oxygen is used by your body to make **energy**.

You need energy to be able to run and play, to get dressed in the morning and to go to the park.

Your body cannot store oxygen, so
it needs fresh supplies all the time.
It does this by breathing in fresh air.

You breathe
in and out all
the time.

Breathing in

When you breathe in, the clean, fresh air goes into your body through your mouth and nose.

The air goes down your throat and into a tube called the windpipe.

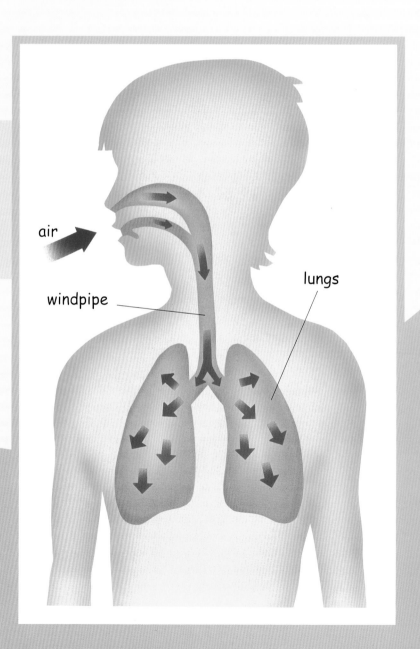

air

windpipe

lungs

The windpipe splits into two tubes and takes air into your lungs.

Your chest gets bigger when you breathe in because your lungs have filled up with air.

Breathing out

When your breathe out, the stale air that has been inside your body is pushed out of your lungs, up your windpipe and back out of your mouth and nose.

Your chest gets smaller when you breathe out, because the stale air has been pushed out of your lungs.

When you play a wind instrument, you must blow into it to make sounds. The harder you blow, the louder the sound.

As air travels through your body, it becomes warm. You can feel the warm air when you put your hand in front of your mouth as you breathe out.

Inside your lungs

There are lots of tiny tubes inside your lungs.
The air that you breathe in passes into the tubes.

The tubes
inside your lungs
split many times
into smaller and
smaller air tubes.
Some are as thin
as a hair.

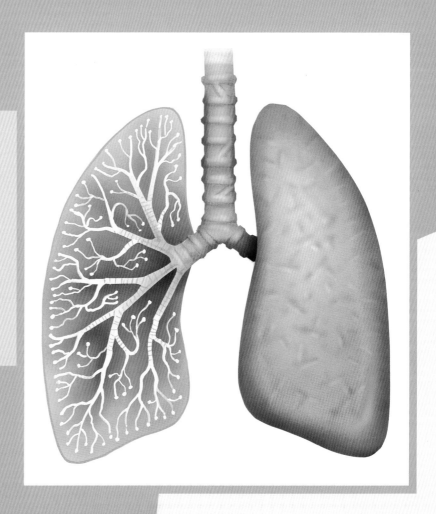

The tubes take the oxygen in the air into your **blood**. The blood carries the oxygen all around your body.

You cannot breathe underwater. To stop your body running out of oxygen, you would need to carry an **air tank**, like this diver.

17

Talking

Your lungs are important for talking as well as for breathing. The air you breathe out goes up your windpipe and through your **voice box** to make sounds.

Shouting uses lots of air. You need to breathe more often when you shout.

Your voice box is in your throat at the top of your windpipe.

A quiet sound, like a whisper, uses less air. Try making different sounds to see how much air you need.

Sometimes when you swallow food, you swallow air as well. A loud burp happens when swallowed air in your stomach comes out in one go.

Out of breath

Sometimes you need extra air. If you need to run because you are late for school, you have to breathe faster and more deeply.

After lots of exercise, you may breathe more than 60 times a minute.

This is because your body needs extra oxygen to give you more energy. Count how many times you breathe in and out for a minute after you have been running.

When you are sitting still, you breathe more slowly because you do not need so much energy.

Coughs and sneezes

When you catch a cold, you cough and sneeze a lot. A cough will help to blow out the wet, sticky liquid called **mucus** in your nose and throat.

Sneezes happen when something tickles your nose. Then the air rushes out of your lungs and comes out of your nose with a huge atishoo.

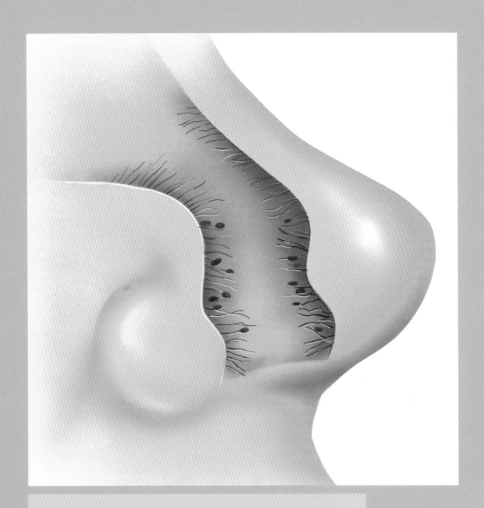

Little hairs inside your nose catch any bits of dust and dirt in the air.

Sometimes dust and dirt floating in the air get inside your throat and lungs. A cough will clear them out.

Breathing problems

Dirty or **polluted air** can cause breathing problems such as **asthma**.

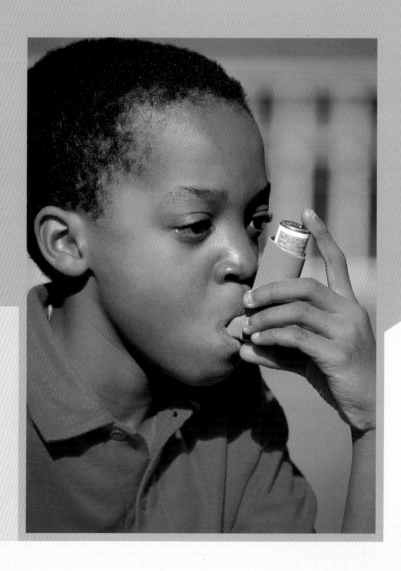

People with asthma carry an inhaler. This pumps medicine into the tubes that carry air into the lungs, to keep them open.

The air in many towns and cities is made dirty by fumes from cars and lorries, and by smoke from factories. Polluted air can damage your lungs.

This girl is wearing a face mask to stop dirty air going into her lungs.

Exercising your lungs

When you run, jump, swim and play games, your lungs take in more air to give your body extra oxygen. This makes your lungs stronger and keeps them healthy.

Roller skating, walking, running and cycling all help to keep your lungs working well.

Your lungs work hard for you all your life, so look after them by taking regular exercise.

Your lungs can be damaged by cigarette smoke. People who smoke often find it hard to breathe and have bad coughs.

Feeling your lungs

You cannot see your lungs, but you can feel them at work. When you breathe in, your lungs get bigger as they fill up with air.

Breathe in and hold your breath for a few seconds. Look at your body.

Now breathe out and see what happens to your body. What do you notice?

When you breathe out, your lungs get smaller as the air is pushed back out of your body. Stand in front of a mirror and try this experiment.

Words to remember

air tank A metal container filled with oxygen, which divers use to breathe under water.

asthma An illness caused by air pollution. When people have asthma, the tubes in their lungs become narrow, making breathing difficult.

blood The red liquid full of oxygen that is pumped around your body by your heart.

bones The hard, tough parts inside your body that make up your skeleton.

breathe To take oxygen from the air into your lungs.

energy The power you need to be able to do all the things you want to do.

inhaler A pump that puffs a special medicine into the air tubes in the lungs.

lungs The soft, spongy parts in your chest that allow you to breathe.

mucus A thick, sticky liquid made by your body. In your nose, it traps dust and dirt and helps keep your lungs clean.

oxygen A gas found in the air that you need in order to breathe.

polluted air Air that is made dirty by the smelly and poisonous gases that come from cars and factories.

ribcage The bones in your chest that protect your lungs.

stale Old and no longer fresh. Stale air is the old air you breathe out after every breath.

voice box The part at the top of your windpipe that makes sounds to allow you to talk.

windpipe The tube in your throat that takes air into your lungs.

Index